1. Dressed for church, *c.* 1900

2. (*overleaf*) Fleet Street, 1897. The railway bridge of the London Chatham and Dover Railway was erected in 1876

Victorian and Edwardian

LONDON

from old photographs

Introduction and commentaries by

JOHN BETJEMAN

B. T. BATSFORD LTD
LONDON

B. T. Batsford Limited,
4 Fitzhardinge St, London W1
Printed in the Netherlands by
Drukkerij De Lange/Van Leer N.V. Deventer
and bound in Great Britain by
Richard Clay (The Chaucer Press) Ltd, Bungay, Suffolk
First published in 1969
Reprinted in 1970
7134 0112 5

CONTENTS

ACKNOWLEDGMENT

Without the kindness and expert knowledge of London librarians, archivists, museum officials and many others this book could not have been produced. For the photographs, the Author and Publishers wish to thank:

Aerofilms Limited for Figs. 30, 32, 48, 54, 108, 110, 128, 155, 159, 170, 174; London Borough of Barnet, Libraries and Arts Committee, for Figs. 191, 192, 198, 199, 200; London Borough of Brent Library Service for Figs. 201, 202, 203; British Railways (Eastern Region) for Fig. 149; British Railways (London Midland Region) for Figs. 142, 150; London Borough of Camden, Libraries and Arts Department for Figs. 193, 194, 196; William Gordon Davis for Figs. 3, 24, 34, 40, 93, 94, 98, 99, 105, 112, 115, 127, 129, 138, 165, 166, 172; London Borough of Ealing, Central Library, for Figs. 183, 184, 185; London Borough of Enfield, Director of Libraries, Arts and Entertainments, for Fig. 206; *Enfield Gazette and Observer*, for Figs. 207, 208; F. Frith and Company Limited, Reigate, for Figs. 8, 13, 19, 23, 41, 42, 44, 45, 47, 49, 107; London Borough of Hammersmith, Fulham Library and Mrs. F. Wrightson (née Dowden), for Fig. 177; London Borough of Hammersmith, Central Library, for Figs. 161, 179, 182; Greater London Council, Photograph Library, for Figs. 113, 121, 145, 173; London Borough of Greenwich, Greenwich Library, Spurgeon Collection, for Figs. 58, 60, 61, 63, 69, 70, 71, 74, 75, 79, 84, 85, 136, 140, 143, 151, 152, 190; London Borough of Greenwich, Woolwich Library, for Fig. 171; Corporation of London, Guildhall Library, for Figs. 9, 28, 33, 39, 144, 160; London Borough of Haringey, Bruce Castle, for Figs. 204, 205; London Borough of Haringey, Hornsey Library, for Fig. 197; London Borough of Haringey, Wood Green Central Library, for Fig. 189; London Borough of Hounslow, Library Services, for Fig. 181; The Council of The Royal Borough of Kensington and Chelsea, Central Library, for Figs. 86, 87, 88; The Council of The Royal Borough of Kensington and Chelsea, Chelsea Library, for Figs. 90, 91, 92; J. G. Links Esq. for Figs. 55, 59, 64, 65, 66, 80, 81, 125; London Transport for Figs. 6, 11, 17, 22, 43, 50, 114, 116, 148, 169, 178, 180, 187, 188; London Borough of Merton, Wimbledon Public Library, for Figs. 168, 175, 176; The Mansell Collection for Figs. 29, 31, 37, 38, 157, 163; Radio Times Hulton Picture Library for Figs. 2, 14, 16, 19, 26, 35, 46, 76, 83, 95, 96, 97, 100, 101, 103, 107, 109, 118, 131, 141, 147, 154, 156, 186; Science Museum, London, for Figs. 4, 5; London Borough of Southwark, Public Libraries, for Figs. 134, 135; London Borough of Tower Hamlets, Libraries Committee, for Figs. 117, 119, 120, 158; The Trustees of the Victoria and Albert Museum, for Figs. 7, 10, 62, 102, 130, 133, 139, 162, 167; London Borough of Wandsworth, West Hill District Library, for Fig. 146; City of Westminster, Public Library, Buckingham Palace Road, for Fig. 52.

The remainder of the photographs are from the Publisher's collection.

The factual information on which the picture commentaries are based has come from published sources and from many individual specialists. In particular grateful acknowledgment is due to Lady Betjeman, Mr. James L. Howgego (of the Guildhall Library), Mr. E. A. Carson (of the Library, Museum and Records of H.M. Customs and Excise), Dr. D. B. Thomas (of the Science Museum), Mr. J. H. Scholes and Mr. R. Elliott (of the Museum of British Transport), Mr. Felix Salmon, Mr. David Leggatt (of the Libraries Department of the London Borough of Greenwich), and the staff of the London Library.

During the two years that the book has been in preparation a vital secretarial link in the collection both of photographs and of information about their subjects has been provided by Miss Mary Scriven.

3. A Hansom in Baker Street, 1900. A patent for the design of the Hansom was taken out by the architect Joseph Hansom in 1834

What a bright sunshiny morning it was, and what fun I had going with John in a Hansom cab to Paddington!—I like a Hansom cab, it goes so fast.

G. J. Whyte Melville, *Kate Coventry*

INTRODUCTION

Selecting the photographs for this book was both pleasant and con-fusing. There were about five times more than are included here. As we arranged them in the first floor back of the publisher's office, putting some on tables and others on the floor until the whole room was awash with photographs, the three selectors, Sam Carr who also did the research and the original hunting up of sources of supply; Brian Batsford who did the layout and I, were the prey of conflicting emotions. Were we to be guided by aesthetic appeal only? Were we to confine our selection to pictures of buildings and streets that had disappeared for ever? Were we to confine them to certain dates? *i.e.* to exclude any photographs showing motorcars, however early, so that we could call the book "Horse-drawn London"? Then, should we arrange the contents chronologically or topographically?

During all the many hours of our looking and sorting and dis-cussing, two things emerged. One was that photography, at any rate, so far as local topography is concerned was not consciously an art. The art has to be in the mind of the selectors except for a few ex-ceptional cases like W. H. Fox Talbot, who consciously composed pictures. Today photography seems to us more truthful than drawing or engraving, more coldly impersonal than Hogarth, more accurate than Loggan and without any of the "artistic liberties" which we suspect of Turner and Whistler. Because we are so used to films and to newspapers with photographs in them, we have come to regard them as more truthful than the printed word—and with some justification.

And all the time there was London. It was outside us and how far did it stretch? It certainly included the City and Westminster, but did it include Middlesex, Essex, Kent and Surrey? And if so, how far did the County of London, that late Victorian invention, extend? Did it include the semi-rurality of what is now called Greater London? Another curious thing we found was that London interpreted entirely in terms of its buildings was dead. The people were as important as the buildings. To take the people entirely on their own would be an over emphasis in one direction. There never has been a general type of Londoner. Londoners are of all sorts of trades and types and classes and nations. In fact, the place is a capital and has been since Elizabethan times. It is also what Raymond Unwin called it "a collection of villages". To this day the people of Bermondsey are most of them lost when they cross to the north bank of the Thames, and the people of Belgravia are equally lost when they reach the Elephant and Castle (and so incidentally are the people of Elephant and Castle, who knew it before it was rebuilt). And though everybody has heard of Soho, not many could tell you what borough it was in, nor would they know whether Mayfair was part of Kensington or Westminster. At any rate they would have to think, because London is what Raymond Unwin said it was. And this collection of villages is not to be thought of entirely in terms of parishes as we do when we get into the English country. It is a series of settlements divided by trade, race and occupation or lack of it.

If there is one thing which is common to all the London that is shown here, it is the sense of streets. London street life was a way of life. The first break up of street life was with the high-minded industrial dwellings erected by the Victorians. Today their modern equivalents are called "point blocks". Except for the disappearance of so many of its streets, London had not greatly changed, even as a result of the internal combustion engine. That is to say the centre of London had not greatly changed. We are less aware of the many hills in London. They have been replaced by slabs of offices and flats.

We are inclined to think that there can never have been such a hellish noise as there is in London now, with motorcars, scooters, low-flying aeroplanes, buses and over-heavy lorries, yet Stephen Coleridge writing in 1913 at the age of close on fifty said: "London

4. Vanished Bridges. (*Above*) Waterloo Bridge, designed by John Rennie, completed in 1831, and demolished in 1935. In the background is Somerset House (Sir William Chambers, architect, 1776), unchanged since this photograph was taken about 1910. (*Below*) Hungerford Bridge. Designed by Isambard Kingdom Brunel and opened in 1845. Destroyed 1860 and its chains used in Clifton Suspension Bridge (opened 1864). The Shot Tower (demolished in 1962) is in the background. The photograph was taken by W. H. Fox Talbot just after the bridge had been opened

has changed very much since I was a boy. All the main streets were paved with stone blocks, and as there were no India rubber tyres, the noise was deafening. In the middle of Regent's Park or Hyde Park, one heard the roar of the traffic all round in a ring of tremendous sound; and in any shop in Oxford Street, if the door was opened no one could make himself heard till it was shut again."

It would have been possible to have made the captions to the photographs in this book into a long lament for what has disappeared.

5. Trafalgar Square. Laid out by Nash in the 1820s, it was originally on a slope, but was re-designed in its present form, 1840, by Sir Charles Barry. Nelson's Column erected 1837–42. The photograph was taken by W. H. Fox Talbot about 1844

But when I look at the noisy muddle at the junctions of Euston Road, Hampstead Road and Tottenham Court Road, at what is now Warren Street Underground Station, as depicted in the photograph (194) and see the faceless efficiency of overpass and underpass churning in its clouds of diesel through the impersonal slabs which are there now, I realise we have only changed one sort of bad for another sort of bad. What we have lost in Central London in many places has been the human element. Buildings and machines have dominated hitherto indomitable cockneys.

Chain stores and multiple office buildings and flats have made many parts of London indistinguishable from their post-war equivalents in Birmingham, Coventry or Exeter. The backgrounds in this book have not the interchangeable quality of modern housing and industrial estates. Here they are undoubtedly London. Those who know their lamp-posts will often be able to tell which borough of London a place is in without having to look at the captions below. It is hard to define the exact London quality which pervades this book. Perhaps the prevalence of brick buildings is part of it, and most of us can recall London stock was used in brick streets from the late eighteenth century until the 1880's. After that red brick and terracotta and gables became the fashion. London is essentially East Anglian and has more in common, so far as building materials are concerned, with Cambridge than Oxford.

The biggest casualty of all has been the County of Middlesex, and the parts of Surrey nearest London. It was a countryside that inspired Keats and Constable—small hills, dairy farms, weatherboarded inns, horse ponds and heaths, and the occasional little Georgian mansions of city merchants who had set up as squires. In the eighteen-sixties Victorian tradesmen built Italianate and Gothic and Swiss mansions on the northern heights of London, or around Sydenham. These make the final pages surprisingly historical for hardly a mansion remains that has not been divided into flats or turned into offices or de-molished, hardly an inn that has not been rebuilt or a garden that has not been filled with little houses.

THE CITY

6. Cheapside, looking east to Bow Church, 1886. Wordsworth's plane tree still stands above the small shops on the left

7. Newgate Gaol, *c.* 1895. George Dance Junior who rebuilt the gaol between 1770–1782, was influenced by Piranesi, the Italian architect-engraver. The design was deliberately sombre and fortress-like, and the blank walls made interesting by rusticated blocks and recesses. Public hangings took place outside the gaol until May 1868

8. Threadneedle Street and the Bank of England, *c.* 1895. Sir John Soane, who rebuilt the Bank of England in 1788–1808, was the pupil of George Dance Junior. He also wanted to create a fortress effect but one which suggested opulence as well. He therefore varied the blank walls with columns and balustrades

9. The Royal Exchange, 1897. Designed by Sir William Tite and rebuilt 1841–1844. It replaced earlier cloistered renaissance buildings on the same site. Merchants and citizens met in the cloisters to discuss business. The use of the Exchange for this purpose died out in the last century until by this century only two or three top-hatted men met in it. Late Victorian and Edwardian frescoes still adorn its covered courtyard

10. Sir Paul Pindar Tavern, Bishopsgate Without, 1875. These houses were demolished in 1890 to make space for an enlargement of Liverpool Street Station. The seventeenth-century bow-window and front of the tavern (itself only a part of Sir Paul Pindar's original mansion) are now in the Victoria and Albert Museum

11. St. Martin-le-Grand, 1896. The Greek style building on the right is the General Post Office which was built by Sir Robert Smirke in 1824–1829 and demolished about 1910. None of the buildings shown here survives

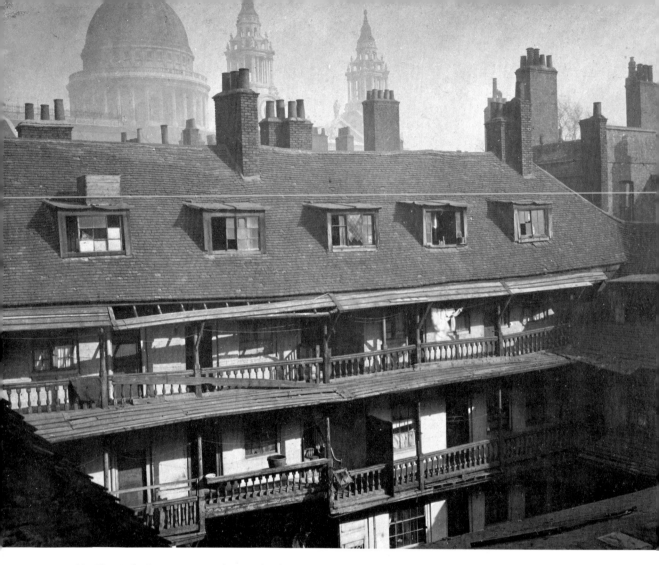

12. The *Oxford Arms*, Warwick Lane (with St. Paul's behind), 1875. This was pulled down in 1876. Warehouses were built on its site. The last of these seventeenth-century galleried London inn yards to remain is the *George*, Southwark

13. London Bridge, *c*. 1890, as designed by John Rennie and his son Sir John in 1831. In 1905 the pavements were corbelled out on either side so as to give more width to the road. Old London Bridge, which had houses on it, was further downstream to the right. The tower of Wren's church of St. Magnus the Martyr was at its entrance on the City bank. This tower has now been obscured by Adelaide House (1924). On the left of the bridge is Fishmongers' Hall, 1831–1834, by Henry Roberts

14. Holborn looking east, *c.* 1895, before the main blocks of the Prudential Assurance Building, 1899–1906, by Alfred Waterhouse had been completed

15. An omnibus and its driver, 1877. The driver, on the left, was a famous employee of Thomas Tilling known as Cast-iron Billy

16. Cabbies, 1877. The driver of the Hansom cabs was able to open the flaps across the seat, to let passengers in or out, by means of a lever on his offside

17. King William Street, 1896. King William IV, by Samuel Nixon (1844), which is seen at the end of the street, was removed to the Royal Naval College, Greenwich, in 1936. This street leads off to the left to the Bank. Just over its houses may be seen the now hidden tower of Wren's St. Clement, Eastcheap

18. "Little Italy", Holborn (Summers Street at right), 1907. So named because there is still a large Italian colony here with their Neapolitan-looking R.C. Church of St. Peter in Clerkenwell Road. Most of the small streets in this district between Clerkenwell Road, Rosebery Avenue and Grays Inn Road were destroyed in favour of grim Industrial Buildings

19. (*overleaf*) "The New Law Courts" and Fleet Street about 1895. The Law Courts by G. E. Street, left, 1868–1882. Temple Bar Monument by Sir Horace Jones, 1880. Fleet Street still consisted largely of old narrow houses. The octagonal tower of St. Dunstan's in the West by John Shaw 1829–1833 is in the distance. A "Knifeboard" horse bus is on right of foreground with outside seats back to back

20. Aldgate Pump, *c.* 1880. The eighteenth-century style pump was where Leadenhall and Fenchurch Streets meet and the City stops and the East End begins

WESTMINSTER

21. Recruiting Sergeants at Westminster, 1877. Where they are standing are now Government offices. St. Margaret's, Westminster, in background. The lamp standards, like the Sergeants, lent dignity to Parliament Square laid out by Sir Charles Barry in the eighteen-fifties

22. Horse-drawn tram at the eastern end of Victoria Street, *c.* 1870. The line was built by George Francis Train and opened in 1861. It was short-lived because of the unpopularity of its raised rails

23. The Strand looking east. Somerset House, right; St. Mary-le-Strand, centre (*c.* 1900). The houses on the left were pulled down at the beginning of the century to make way for the Aldwych–Kingsway scheme. Holywell Street and Wych Street were between St. Mary-le-Strand and St. Clement Danes and were famous for second-hand book shops. The Strand was much narrower, as appears on the right of the view

24. The Aldwych and, at right, the Gaiety Theatre, 1909, replaced the old houses bottom left. The outside of the Gaiety was by Norman Shaw, 1902–1903, and it was destroyed in the 1950s

THE STRAND

25. The Strand, Charing Cross Station at right, *c.* 1900. None of the buildings on the right remains

26. Charing Cross at Craven Street, *c*. 1900. The building on the right between Craven Street and the entrance to Charing Cross Railway Terminus was replaced in 1915 by Lyons Strand Corner House, designed by F. J. Wills

CHARING CROSS

27. Northumberland House and Charles I statue. Northumberland House, the town mansion of the Duke of Northumberland, was built in *c*. 1605 and demolished in 1874. The street in which it stood is now Northumberland Avenue. Whitehall is on the right and faced by Le Sueur's Charles I statue (1633)

28. Pall Mall East and the National Gallery, *c.* 1895. The National Gallery by William Wilkins, 1832-1838, was designed to be seen sideways on, as it appears here from Pall Mall. All the late Georgian buildings in the foreground have been destroyed except the portico, on the right, of what is now Canada House

29. Trafalgar Square, *c.* 1905. The Golden Cross Hotel, long known as Morley's Hotel, on the left was a stucco late-Georgian building of *c.* 1825. It was destroyed early in the 1930s to make way for South Africa House. Grand Buildings in the middle of the photograph are still here and date from the eighteen-seventies. They were once the Grand Hotel

30. Big Ben in 1897. Then statues, lamp-posts and ornamental ironwork were a foreground to the Palace of Westminster and the Abbey. The area was originally laid out in 1868

31. The Embankment, looking to Cleopatra's Needle and Somerset House, *c.* 1900. On the left the Cecil Hotel (1886) where Arnold Bennett stayed and which was more fashionable than its neighbour the Savoy (where Claude Monet used to stay). The Cecil was destroyed in 1930 to make way for Shell Mex House. The Embankment, built 1864–1870, cuts off the hitherto wide slow-flowing Thames from the houses on its banks

32. Whitehall and Parliament Street, *c.* 1895. The houses on the right were destroyed at the beginning of this century to make way for the New Government Offices when Parliament Street was widened

33. Piccadilly Circus looking east, *c.* 1880. Opposite is Coventry Street going into Leicester Square. The tall dark building on the right is the Criterion designed by Thomas Verity in 1874 and reconstructed in 1904. The original circus is still discernible to right and left

34. Piccadilly Circus from the south end of the Quadrant, 1900. The Circus has now disappeared. The Criterion is on the right. The London Pavilion (1885) on the left and Sir Alfred Gilbert's Eros of 1892 recall that once there was a circle of buildings here

PICCADILLY CIRCUS

35. Piccadilly Circus: London Pavilion at back, *c.* 1899. The London Pavilion was built in 1885 but was for so long covered with advertisements that people had forgotten what it looked like. The elegant cast-iron, many-lamp-posted public lavatories in the middle ceased to challenge Eros when the new Piccadilly Circus underground station was built in the late 1920s

36. Leicester Square and the Empire, 1895. The Empire was destroyed in January 1927. The photograph was taken by Paul Martin

37. Hyde Park Corner, *c.* 1900. The houses beyond Apsley House on the left were destroyed in the Hyde Park "Improvement" Scheme in the 1960s

38. Piccadilly; the Green Park at right, *c.* 1900. The cab shelter has gone. So have the late Georgian houses on the left. The gap, which is the forecourt of Devonshire House (demolished 1924), shows the Berkeley beyond. Opposite, on the right, is now the Ritz Hotel (1906)

39. Piccadilly looking towards Burlington House (right), 1890. The Bath Hotel is the stucco building on the right. It was demolished *c.* 1905. Piccadilly was a street of individual small and long-established shops rather as Jermyn Street, Bond Street and the bottom of St. James's and the side streets off Piccadilly are to-day

40. Piccadilly: the Egyptian Hall (P. J. Robinson, 1811–1812), 1895. The Hall was at 170/171 Piccadilly, a short distance to the east of St. James's Street. It was demolished in 1905

41. Park Lane looking towards Marble Arch, *c.* 1895. The Dorchester Hotel and Grosvenor House occupy the site on the right

PARK LANE

42. (*overleaf*) Park Lane near Marble Arch, *c.* 1895. Amongst those living then in the houses seen overleaf were: James Hall Renton (at No 39), George Murray Smith (at No 40), Sir Henry Bruce Meux Bart (at No 41), Vice-Admiral Robert O'Brien Fitzroy (at No 42), The Hon Aubrey Fitz Clarence (at No 43), and the Duke of Cambridge (at No 44)

43. Marble Arch and Oxford Street, 1896. The Marble Arch was thought of as a North-East entrance to Hyde Park. Moved to its present position in 1851, it had originally stood in front of Buckingham Palace. It was in scale with the buildings round when Oxford Street, at this, its western end, was still partly residential

44. Oxford Street looking east from near the present side of Selfridge's (at left), *c.* 1895

45. Oxford Street looking towards Oxford Circus, *c.* 1900

46. Oxford Street at Regent Circus, *c.* 1900. This later became known as "Oxford Circus". It was part of John Nash's grand scheme of a processional way leading from The Regent's Park down Portland Place, through to Piccadilly and thence down the hill to Waterloo Place and St. James's Park

47. Oxford Street looking East, between Oxford Circus and Tottenham Court Road (*Theodora* is on at the Princess's Theatre so that the date is 1890)

48. The Alhambra, Leicester Square, 1899

49. Regent Street, looking south from Oxford Circus, *c.* 1910. John Nash's scheme of the 1820s dominated the west end of London, dividing Soho from the Hanover Square district

REGENT STREET

50. Regent Street: the Quadrant, 1884. There was a covered Colonnade of cast-iron columns along either side of this quadrant. It sheltered shoppers and gave proportion to the street. It was destroyed in 1848

51. Regent Street: The Café Royal, *c.* 1910. In at those doors went artists and writers from the days of Oscar Wilde and Beardsley to those of Augustus John. When Nash's Regent Street was demolished by the Crown Commissioners in the 1920s (the Piccadilly Hotel of 1905–1908 by Norman Shaw was the beginning of the trouble) and higher buildings erected so as to bring in more rent, the scale was destroyed

52. Regent Street: the International Fur Store, *c.* 1900. A certain reticence was still maintained in shop frontages. In order not to blot out the Georgian stucco above, the ironwork signs are transparent

53. Tottenham Court Road. Right, site of Dominion Theatre, *c.* 1885. Public houses such as the *Horse Shoe* on the right and the long-demolished tavern on the left, always had private gas lanterns bracketed out above their ground floors

54. Posters of the late 'Nineties. John Hassall designed the poster for *The Only Way*; Dudley Hardy for *A Gaiety Girl*

55. "Bill-Stickers", 1877. The small poster which is being pasted advertises a new
waxwork at Madame Tussaud's of "William Fish, The Blackburn Murderer"

STREET TRADERS

56. A Flower Girl (in Cheapside), 1892

There are many sad and weary,
  In this pleasant land of ours,
Crying ev'ry night so dreary,
  "Won't you buy my pretty flowers"
                                    —A. W. French

57. "Strawberries, All Ripe! All Ripe!", 1877

58. A Hokey-Pokey (Ice Cream) Stall, Greenwich, 1884

Hokey-Pokey
Penny a lump,
That's the stuff
To make you jump

59. Italian Ice Cream Seller, 1877

60. Muffin Man, 1885

61. Rabbit-Seller, Greenwich, 1884

62. Sherbet and Water, in the City, *c.* 1895

63. A Ginger-Cake Seller, Greenwich, 1884

65. A Chair-Mender, 1877

66. Street Locksmith, 1877

64. (*opposite*) St. Giles: Cheap Fish
Stall, 1877

67. Water Cart, 1877

68. Knife Grinder, 1884

69. Flower and Plant Cart, Greenwich, 1885

70. Cat's Meat Man, Greenwich, 1885

71. Milkman, Greenwich, 1885

72. (*overleaf*) Newsvendors, Ludgate Circus, 1892

73. Boot-black, 1895

74. Sweep, 1884

My name it is Sam Hall, chimney sweep
My name it is Sam Hall,
I robs both great and small,
But they makes me pay for all—
    Damn their eyes.

—W. G. Ross

75. Match Seller, 1884
Bryant and May's Alpine Vesuvians (Brimstone Matches, they were called) were long-headed, slow-burning fusees which could not be blown out by the wind

76. Postman, *c.* 1900

77. Covent Garden Flower Sellers, 1877

78. "Boardman", 1877. Renovo was a patent
cleaner for fabrics

The photographs of Street Traders and Street Entertainers come, with one or two exceptions, either from J. Thomson
and Adolphe Smith, *Street Life in London*, 1877 (where the illustrations are actual photographic prints); or from a
series of lantern slides made about 1884 for a Greenwich Baptist Minister, the Reverend Charles Spurgeon (a son of
the Revivalist preacher).

STREET ENTERTAINERS

79. A Barrel Organ Player, 1884

If you saw my little backyard wot a pretty spot you'ld cry
It's a picture on a sunny summer day
With the turnip tops and cabbages wot people don't buy
I makes it on a Sunday look all gay.
Oh it really is a verry pretty garden
And Chingford to the eastward could be seen
Wiv a ladder and some glasses, you could see to 'Ackney Marshes
If it wasn't for the 'ouses in between
—Words by Edgar Bateman, sung by Gus Elen

80. "Fifth of November Effigy", 1877

81. Italian Street Musicians, 1877

82. Dancing Bear, 1895

83. An Organ Grinder, 1895 (*Photographer: Paul Martin*)

84. Black-face Minstrels, 1884

Wheel about, and turn about
And do just so;
Ebry time I wheel about
I jump Jim Crow

85. "Promenade Concert", 1884

KENSINGTON AND CHELSEA

86. Outside Harrods, Knightsbridge, *c.* 1905. Harrods Store 1901–1905 was designed by Stevens and Munt. It is in terra-cotta to tone in with the fashionable Hans Town and Cadogan Square which are south of it

87. Kensington Church Street, *c.* 1905

88. High Street, Kensington, looking east, *c.* 1905

89. Westbourne Grove, 1900. Whiteley's on the right was rebuilt 1908–1912

90. Chelsea Old Church from Battersea Bridge, *c.* 1870
The Embankment, which was designed by Sir Joseph Bazalgette, was constructed here 1871–1874, just after this photograph was taken

91. Cheyne Walk looking east towards the Albert Bridge (before the Embankment was built), *c.* 1870

92. Cheyne Walk looking west towards Chelsea Old Church (before the Embankment was built), *c.* 1870

The photographs on these two pages were taken by John Hedderley. Originally a Chelsea grainer and sign-writer, Hedderley by 1869 had become a full-time photographer

93. A Hansom Cab outside the Albert Hall, 1900
The fares for Hansoms were two shillings for four miles from Charing Cross,
and double rate beyond. When hired by time the rates were a minimum of
two shillings and sixpence per hour, and eightpence per quarter hour thereafter

HOW THE RICH LIVED

94. On the ice in St. James's Park, 1875

95. (*overleaf*) Church Parade in Rotten Row, *c.* 1902

96. A meeting of the Four-in-Hand Club, Rotten Row, *c.* 1895

Of all the delights in the world give me my morning canter up the park on Brilliant. Away we go, understanding each other perfectly; and I am quite sure that he enjoys as much as I do the bright sunshine, and the morning breeze, and the gleaming Serpentine, with its solitary swan, and its hungry ducks, and its amphibious dogs
—G. J. Whyte Melville, *Kate Coventry*

97. Carriages in Hyde Park, *c.* 1895

We were spanking round the park behind Ready and Rhino. Miss Phaeton's horses are very large; her groom is very small, and her courage is indomitable. . . .

"Were you ever in love?" she asked, just avoiding a brougham which contained the Duchess of Dexminster. (If, by the way, I have to run into any one, I like it to be a Duchess: you get a much handsomer paragraph)
—Anthony Hope, *The Dolly Dialogues*

98. Hyde Park on Sunday morning, 1901

99. The Ladies Archery Club, Kensington Gardens, 1900

100. (*opposite*) A Charity Matiné
the Haymarket Theatre, 1899

101. Lord's: Luncheon Interval at the Eton and Harrow Match, 1895. The game ended in "a draw, greatly in favour of Eton"

102. At the "Earl's Court County Sale", 1902

103. An electric brougham in Lower Regent Street, *c*. 1905. The German flag is waving on its then popular Embassy and the Duke of York surveys a St. James's Park as yet unscored with straight lines by Sir Aston Webb.

Life was a railway journey; foes and friend,
Infected with nostalgy of the end,
Awaited patiently the crack of doom;
But thank the powers that be, the motor boom,
Predestined to postpone the judgment-day,
Arrived in time to show a better way.

—John Davidson

THE PARKS

104. A photographer on Clapham Common, 1877. A wet-plate field camera is being used.

105. The Round Pond, Kensington Gardens, 1896

106. In Victoria Park, *c.* 1900. Victoria Park was laid out in 1842 in a romantic landscape style by Sir James Penne-thorne, the architect (*Photographer: Paul Martin*)

107. (*opposite*) In Hyde Park, *c.*

On the new velocipede so gail
You'll see the people riding do
Everyone should try one, ever
should buy one,
See the new velocipede
—Frank W. G

108. Skating at Sydenham (Crystal Palace), *c.* 1900. The Prehistoric Monsters (of which one appears in the background) were added to the Crystal Palace grounds in 1854

109. The Zoo, 1900. (*Photographer: Paul Martin*)

110. The Lily Pond at Sydenham, *c*. 1900

111. ''Mush-Fakers'' and Ginger-Beer Sellers on Clapham Common, 1877. A mush-faker was an umbrella mender

THE EAST END

112. The Ratcliff Highway, Stepney, 1896

113. (*overleaf*) Providence Place, Stepney, c. 1909

114. Shoreditch High Street, 1896. The horse-tram lines are in the cobbles

115. (*opposite*) East End school children starting for a day's outing in the country, 1900

116. Whitechapel Road, 1896, with a horse-tram passing what is now the London Hospital

117. Whitechapel High Street, *c.* 1890 (the shops are on the site of Whitechapel Art Gallery, built in 1900)

118. Lamp-post swinging, 1892.
(*Photographer: Paul Martin*)

119. Bethnal Green Road, 1905

Strolling so happy down Bethnal Green
This gay youth you might have seen
Tompkins and I, with his girl between
   Oh what a surprise!
I praised the Conservatives frank and free
Tompkins got angry so speedilee
All in a moment he handed to me
   Two lovely black eyes
          —Charles Coborn, Music Hall Song

120. East India Dock Road, 1904. Horse-trams and a horse-bus and waiting growlers, Poplar (North London Railway) Station

121. Poplar: Yarrow and Hedley's Shipbuilding Yard on the Isle of Dogs, *c.* 1870. Steam launches are being built

122. "Before the Excursion", c. 1895

HOW THE LESS RICH LIVED

123. Old Clothes Shop, Seven Dials, 1877. Shaftesbury Avenue, named after the ninth Earl, the social reformer, and Charing Cross Road were driven through the slums of St. Giles between 1855 and 1887. Pockets of them remained till 1950

124. Road repairs, New Bridge Street, the City, 1892

125. (*opposite*) Outside the Pub, 1877

126. Chambermaids at the First Avenue Hotel, *c.* 1900. The First Avenue Hotel was in High Holborn and flourished between 1881 and 1931

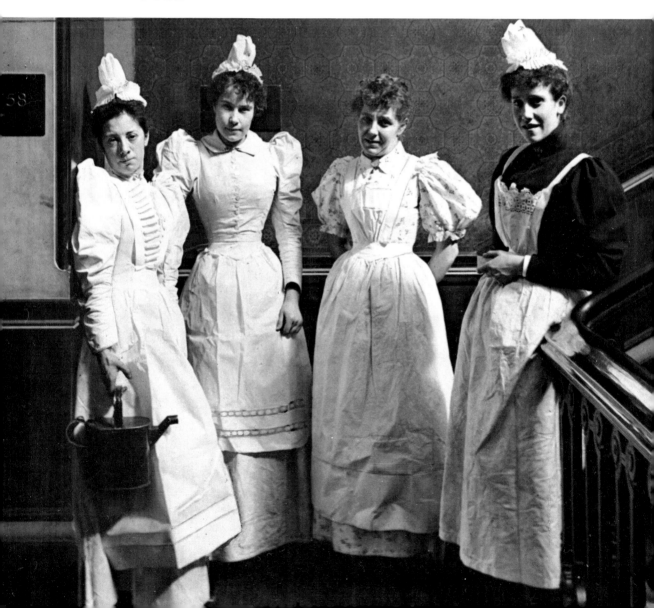

127. On Hampstead Heath, 1910

128. Children, *c*. 1895

129. Tramps in the Green Park, 1900

SOUTH OF THE RIVER

130. A Fair beside Battersea Park, 1892

131. (*overleaf*) A London slum of the 'Eighties

132. Looking to Putney Parish Church from the, now demolished, wooden Fulham Bridge, 1881. Three years later the present Putney Bridge was built

133. Lambeth Palace, *c.* 1895. The paddle-steamer was built in 1864 as the *Citizen D* of the Citizen Steamboat Co. and renamed *Daisy* in 1895 when she had become the property of Victoria Steamboat Association Limited, once rivals of the General Steam Navigation Company Limited. The *Shamrock* (disappearing left) was built for the London Steamboat Company in 1882 at Battersea

134. Duke Street, London Bridge, Southwark Cathedral in background, *c.* 1865. The brick arches on the left carried the Southern Railway, then the South Eastern Railway, on from London Bridge Station past Southwark Cathedral vaguely seen in the distance, to Waterloo Junction and Charing Cross. The rammers were used for the wood blocks

135. The Borough High Street, *c.* 1890

136. Clapham Tram Terminus, Clapham Cross, 1885. Clapham High Street is to the left, on its right the spire (demolished in the Blitz) of the Nonconformist Church. To the right is Clapham Park Road. The photograph was taken from the first floor of the *Plough* Inn

137. Playtime at a board school (schools free and open to all run by local authorities), 1900

138. Punch and Judy, 1900, Trinity Square, Southwark

139. Lambeth: Church Street, 1866. This street later became Lambeth Road

140. Grove Street Fire Station, Blackheath Hill, 1885. The man on the left is the turn-cock, whose job was to turn on the water mains supply ready for the firemen's hoses

141. At the bottom of Ludgate Hill, *c.* 1902: the railway bridge

·*I couldn't touch a stop and turn a screw*
    And set the blooming world a-work for me,
Like such as cut their teeth—I hope, like you—
    On the handle of a skeleton gold key;
I cut mine on a leek, which I eat it every week:
    I'm a clerk at thirty bob as you can see.
                            —John Davidson

THE RAILWAYS

142. St. Pancras Station Hotel in 1876. Architect, Sir Gilbert Scott

143. The London, Brighton and South Coast Railway Co.'s side, *c.* 1882. A D-class tank engine (designed by William Stroudley) is shunting carriages alongside a London and North Western train for Willesden Junction

VICTORIA STATION

144. The exterior, *c.* 1890. Except for the traffic very little has changed

145. Platforms, *c.* 1890. Shunting carriages is a D-class tank engine

CLAPHAM JUNCTION

146. The Approach (on the right, the Horse Tram Depot), *c.* 1900

147. The Metropolitan Railway before its official opening, 1862. William Ewart Gladstone, then Chancellor of the Exchequer, is on the right of the man wearing the white top hat

148. Earl's Court Station, 1896

149. Liverpool Street Station: workmen travelling by the 12.55 p.m. train to Enfield Town. Photograph taken on 25 October, 1884

150. Marylebone Station (Great Central Railway) just after its opening in 1899. Monsignor Ronald Knox said that this was the only London Terminus in which one could hear birdsong. The Great Central Railway was the last, as it was the most sumptuous, trunk line to reach London

151. West Brompton Station, 1876. The engine, a 4-4-OTs, had been introduced twelve years earlier. It came to be used exclusively on the District Railway, and widely on the Metropolitan

152. The Head Guard on the South Eastern Railway (1885). The engine is one of Richard Christopher Mansell's "Gunboat" 0-4-4 tanks, built for Greenwich, Woolwich and Blackheath local services

THE THAMES

153. The crew of a barge on the River, 1877

154. (*overleaf*) At the Docks: unloading a merchantman, *c.* 1885. She is a three-masted barque with an iron hull

155. Under construction, *c.* 1894

TOWER BRIDGE

156. The Opening Ceremony, 30 June, 1895. The architect was Sir Horace Jones, the City Architect. The engineer was Sir John Wolfe Barry, a son of Sir Charles Barry, architect of the Houses of Parliament. The idea of a bascule bridge was Sir Horace's

157. The Tower and Thames lighters photographed from Horsleydown, *c.* 1890

158. The South-West India Dock, *c.* 1875: clipper ships attended by lighters

159. A sailing barge on Greenwich Reach, *c.* 1895. In the background is Greenwich Hospital. A couple of sailing barges were employed by Cory Brothers, the wharfingers, until World War II

160. Paddle steamers at Greenwich Pier, *c.* 1890. The ships are the *Bridegroom* and *Wedding Ring* of the London Steamboat Company, built in 1878 and engaged on short pier-to-pier trips

161. The University Boat Race, 1892, with Oxford three-quarters of a length in the lead. The crews are passing the *Doves* and *Queen's Elm* on Chiswick Reach. Oxford went on to win by two and a quarter lengths

162. A Billingsgate fish porter, 1894

MARKETS

163. Covent Garden Porters, 1877

164. Smithfield Meat Market, *c.* 1895. The architect was Sir Horace Jones, 1866

165. Islington Market, 1904. The Central tower of the Metropolitan Cattle Market (1855), whose base is seen in the background on the left, still survives among new flats on the site. It is by J. Bunning, the City Architect

166. Leadenhall Market, 1897, for poultry. Rebuilt in 1881 by Sir Horace Jones, the City Architect. It is little changed in appearance today

167. In the New Cut Market, Lambeth, 1890

THE SOUTHERN SUBURBS

168. In Merton Road, Wimbledon, *c.* 1910. The tram was electric,
worked from an overhead cable

169. A Thomas Tilling horse-bus outside Raynes Park Hotel, 1903

170. Upper Norwood: parade of the Ancient Order of Foresters down Westow Hill, *c.* 1900

171. Woolwich: Holy Trinity Church, Beresford Square, *c.* 1904. This church, built in 1833, by the gate of the Arsenal, was destroyed in 1962

172. (*overleaf*) The Crystal Palace, Sydenham, 1896. The Crystal Palace was moved here from Hyde Park and opened in Sydenham in 1854. The towers which flanked it were added later

173. The Crystal Palace: the nave, looking north, *c.* 1890. By 1913 the Crystal Palace had ceased to pay as an entertainment centre of South London. It was burned down in 1936

The World compelling plan was thine*—
And, lo! the long laborious miles,
A Palace; lo the giant aisles
Rich in model and design

—Tennyson, 1862

* Prince Albert

174. Bostock and Wombwell's Menagerie at the Crystal Palace, *c.* 1895. Until the Palace was burned down in 1936, Brock's firework displays were held on the slope below it in the summer

> . . . *that fane unique,*
> *Victorian temple of commercialism,*
> *Our very own eighth wonder of the world,*
> *The Crystal Palace.*
> —John Davidson, *c.* 1909

175. A picnic at Caesar's Well, on the Common, *c.* 1905

176. Looking down the High Street, *c.* 1905

THE WESTERN SUBURBS

177. J. Dowden, chimney sweep, with his son, in Fulham Park Gardens, 1893

178. Shepherd's Bush, 1903. The London United tramways departed hence to Uxbridge on the right and to Twicken-ham and Hampton Court to the left, *"clicking under their overhead wires through the rich orchard and farm land of Middlesex, which was just being covered with houses."* (Clark Normanby)

179. Trams at the east end of Shepherd's Bush Green, *c.* 1899

180. Whit Monday, Shepherd's Bush Green. The photographer recorded that the picture was taken at 2.32 p.m. on 23 May, 1903

181. Chiswick High Road, *c.* 1900. Taken from the south side in front of Gunnersbury Station

182. Hammersmith Broadway looking east down Hammersmith Road, *c.* 1905

183. Ealing Broadway, *c.* 1890

184. Ealing: fire engines outside the Town Hall, *c.* 1900

185. Ealing: Broomfield Road from Mattock Lane, 1881

THE NORTHERN SUBURBS

186. An Italian ice cream cart on Hampstead Heath, 1892. (*Photographer: Paul Martin*)

Oh! Oh! Antonio Oh!
Then he's gone away
Left me a-lone-i-o,
All on my own-i-o.

187. King's Cross, 1901. Reggiori's Restaurant on the right has disappeared

188. City Road, Islington, 1890. Pentonville Road is straight ahead and on the corner of the next street is the *Angel* public house

189. Alexandra Palace, Muswell Hill, 1902. It was opened in 1873 as North London's answer to Sydenham's Crystal Palace. In the middle distance is the Ally Pally Racecourse known as "The Frying Pan"

190. A steam tram at Stamford Hill, 1885. Run by the North London Tramways Co., the service went under steam only until 1891

191. Child's Hill: the Castle, *c.* 1905 on the Finchley Road.

192. Hampstead: the *Bull and Bush*, c. 1894

193. Hampstead: the High Street, c. 1895

194. (*overleaf*) Hampstead Road: the south end where it joins Euston Road, 1904. None of this remains

195. Highgate: the *Archway Tavern* at the foot of Highgate Hill, *c.* 1890

196. Highgate Hill and the Archway. From a stereoscope picture of *c.* 1845. The Archway was built by John Nash, 1812–1813, and demolished 1894–1895

197. Highgate: the Public Library (*c.* 1905) is the first house on the left in Shepherd's Hill opposite

198. Hendon: The Pond ("Burrough's Pond"), *c.* 1900. The pond used to be in the Burroughs near its present junction with Watford Way. The eighteenth-century houses in the photograph still survive

199. Hendon: the *Grey Hound* Inn, *c.* 1890. It still stands beside the Parish church of St. Mary, on a height looking miles over Middlesex. But it was rebuilt in the present century

200. Edgware: the High Street and Handel's Smithy, *c*. 1885

201. Kilburn: the Toll Gate, 1860

202. Willesden: the *White Hart*, *c.* 1895: the start of a Bean Feast. From left to right: market cart, gig, wagonette, trap

203. Harlesden: the *Crown* Inn, June 1877

204. Walthamstow: the *Ferry Boat* Inn and River Lea, 1865

205. Tottenham: a horse-bus outside the *Rose and Crown*, 1865. All these houses have disappeared. On the left is Tottenham High Cross which was restored in 1809 and later

206. Winchmore Hill: outside the station (Great Northern Railway), *c.* 1900

207. Waltham Cross during the road widening of 1885

208. Enfield: the *Stag, c.* 1886. The inn was destroyed some five years after this photograph was taken